Spear of Stars

Spear of Stars

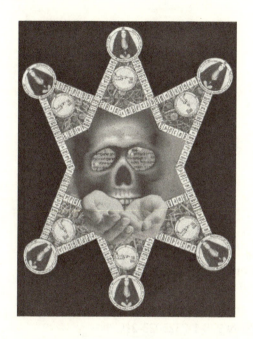

Jason O'Toole

The Red Salon
2018

Spear of Stars
Copyright © 2018 Jason O'Toole
All rights reserved.

ISBN 978-1-7325023-2-1

Cover art: "The Greater Keys of Solomon 42"
by Robert Joseph Barry
Interior art by Jason O'Toole
Biography photo by Laura Goodridge

The Red Salon
PO Box 354
West Union, WV 26456

Contents

In Spring	3
A Witch Executed	4
Mid-Century Maudlin	7
The Innocent	9
The Marker	12
Freya Waits	14
Against Her Nature	17
Spear of Stars	19
The Apocalypse of Little Jack Horner	21
Half a Star	22
Jim of the Roses	24
The Cyclist	26
Junkyard Song	28
Nothing on Earth	30
Go Street	32
The Jackal and the Centipede	34
Last This Century	35
Baby Grand	36
So Below	37
Bluebeard	38
Hellbender	42

Rags	44
Plan "B"	45
Damn the Dream	46
Life Like	47
I Left	48
Sueños de Homicida	49
World without Saints	51
Hail the Coffin King!	53
Spring into Being	60
Biography	65

In Spring

The archer
His handpicked assassin
Stalks the child
Through the woods
She dies
Under a very old tree
She dies
Choking on crushed pearls

Her doppelgänger emerges
Feasting on human hearts
Devouring sentiment

It is Spring!
In every flower's bloom
A grinning death's head
Another shot at Eden

What a lovely spot
For a battlefield

A Witch Executed

In memory of Deborah Babcock Hoxsie, my 6th great-grandmother, put to death by drowning. This sentence was carried out on February 3, 1761 in Providence, RI, 68 years after the supposed witches and wizards of Salem Village met their fate.

Shot with silver sleeve button
Flew limping through the flax
No more would that pestiferous wood hare
Perturb our gardens

Elsewhere, that wagging tongued widow
Collapsed clutching
At her hind
In which the village surgeon
Did find
That self-same missile

Down shadeless lanes
Driven in chains
Through obdurate doors of that temple
Where no lie can hide
Met her blameless accusers

How her familiar spirits

Deranged pewter dishes
Dulled knives, sharpened spoons
Polluted milk-pans with green-eyed flies

To goodwives taught unhallowed charms
Lustily they surrendered
To ravening Lucifer's arms
Their errors bore in hard wombs

Or birthed monsters
Whose last breath we stole away
To alay
Heaven

Dread philters she brewed
Would cause when quaffed
Prayers punctuated with sepulchral cough
Children nursed with tampered chalice
Tiny souls carried off to Moloch's palace.
Backwards recited Scripture
From their quivering lips

One knows paranormals hate iron
As they love Hell
She caused mares to throw their shoes
Striking men dead where they stood

Her own mount
Rode smooth shod
Over the pallid snow

Two-handed stones she conjured
Each thaw up from Hades
No end to cursed stones
On which plowshares cracked
Into cairns and low walls
Crisscrossing tree-rid fields stacked

Her stripped garment on the ground
We searched and found
The marks of her pledge to the master
She, like Peter
Denied

From a locust tree she hung
Her body we flung
as silver from Judas' black hand
Into fields she made infertile

Know then
We are spotless
Who heeded His Word

Mid Century Maudlin

Shroud of greyed flannel
Wore self to shadow
Banished as the sun
Draws water

Sink into hardwoods
Slink from oak liquor
Cabinet to rosewood coffin

This is a place I come often

Under beam and post
Tied to a tulip
Chair with my
Children's entrails
No loyal hand catches venom
I face alone
Roots and bark
A glass of bitters
An eyeful of splinters

Shrinking gods left us
On Pentecost
How we tried to follow!

Pigeons ate their
Trail of crumbs

It was a witch age
In those dark woods
We killed the huntsman
Pushed the hag into
Her own smoking oven

The truth is there was
No chicken bone only
Famine's finger
And I am not a child
Filling pockets with
Pure white pebbles
In my grim tale I am
The plywood cutter
Can't blame step-mother

No white swan comes
To bring my children home

The Innocent

For Jane O.

Watching my daughter play chase
With a dragonfly
Under the unforgiving Georgia sun
How her sweet milk complexion glowed
Her copper wire hair shone

A giggling game
Between girl and double-winged hunter
Tiny feet dodging fire ant mounds
Scaring dutiful bumble bees off their clovers
They played until sundown

Five summers passed
My daughter met me coming up the steps
Matter-of-factly informing
"There's a fairie in the woods."

A ruby throated hummingbird?
A lunar moth? Oh of course,
A dragonfly?

Smiling, she turned to face the treeline and

Called in sing-song
"Fairie, come out!"

In that hushed moment butterflies froze mid-air
Robins and worms ceased their tug-o-war
Time slipped the shackles of gravity

A blue-bodied figure
No larger than the head of a daisy
Flew a gentle arc
Over the top of an untended pecan grove
Wings a blur
Delicate limbed with featureless face
Vibrating at a foreign frequency
She circled our heads
In voiceless benediction
Pausing only for a moment
Between my eyes
So I too would see
And believe

As speedily as she appeared
Back into the cathedral of leaf and twig she returned
Darting through fragrant honeysuckle

Again in our own time

Familiar sounds returned to the dew heavy air
Mockingbirds mimicking Thrashers
Dalmatian begging to return
To her Wild Hunt
Squealing axels of flatbeds
Hauling lumber

Of this enchantment
We never spoke again
In time
Careless time
We never spoke at all
In my sickness
I chose a bottle over you
In turn
You withdrew from me
Into your own frowning forest

Do you remember that merry summer visitor
Who welcomed us behind her fluttering veil?
Does that dreamworld still wait
As I
For your innocent song to call it back?

The Marker

For James O.

This memory
Have I whittled it down
With thought or
Have my fears
Compressed it to a speck

Always at my center
I may be hollow
I am not empty

Don't expect your gratitude
When you fearlessly sleep
Through coyotes' piercing howls
For your sharp axe
And sharper knife
Or when you warm your tired hands
By your own fire

Perhaps though
When you break camp
And leave the forest
Remember the man

Who once walked with you

As for me
An ancient ash
Waits at my trail's end
For me and my knife
With which I will carve
A solitary dot
Forever enclosed in a circle

Freya Waits

Red feathered wings
Outspread more luminous
Than any earthly crown
Give glory to the sun

She weaves purest light
Her spindle
A tall, white birch
Slow and sure
Even as the baleful March wind
Knifes the air
Between us

Battering the branches
This wind speaks of spring
To Mother birch
Her naked silvery fingers
Through playful legerdemain
Interlace to form ciphers
Speaking to my inner-eye
A parable of endurance

Her papery bark peels back
Into sacred scrolls

Dropping to earth
For those who might read them

Her companion selects a perch
And waits
In her cloak she is this day
A hawk
There will come another time
When she will carry me away
To that great hall of our fathers
I will add my shield
To that mighty roof

How I long to go
Though I beg a bit more time
My battle wounds were fatal
Though slowly they take me down
More time!
To win back all that is lost
Not with roguish swindles
Nor force
How then?

In patience I must wait
For answers to appear
As seasons pass and boughs

Reach Skyward
Twisting out wisdom
For the few
Who will know

Against Her Nature

When the carpet is pulled up
& the bodies are found
Reddened Runes cast
Hexes drawn

When the floorboards come up
& the bodies are found
Strange maths seen
Bones sawn

She tears at my face
To make the human race
Pay for all the crimes
Against her nature

I have no home
Except what's inside me
My tribe is dying
I drive from mansion to tent
Workers sweat under conquering sun
To repair the back of the serpent

When the floor is torn up
& the bodies are found

Sick sigils show
A hand of glory

When the house comes down
& the bodies are found
A helm of awe
In her book of mirrors

Now the serpent healed
Grasps her tail
& prepares to let go
But I am already cast off
Into my own twilight

Spear of Stars

She dreams of her earths
On this, our earth
She keeps a husband
Called Night
She lights his pipe
With a spark of silence
He dips his bread
Into a bowl of blood
She reclines like a sunset
She is all sunsets
& the light that makes shadow
In the morning she melts his teeth of ice

On another earth she makes it rain diamonds
Which slice the eyes of storms
There are no donkeys carrying kings
No messianic signs
No false gods to destroy
No fool to shout
"Not Her, but I"

One earth, the first and last
She hides in her belly
Not a babe to be born

No sphere
A web of scars
Pierced as she was by her spear of stars

The Apocalypse of Little Jack Horner

In your cold corner
Broken, incomplete and you!
You once burned so brightly
Now your song a weak whisper
Tempts her not

It is for me to take your place
I warm her face and illuminate
Her beauty for all to admire
The flowers grow under my command
For her and her gentle feet
Do no harm

I burn the fog away
The murkiness shudders and clears at my name
The wet dew shivers on each blade of grass
On every leaf
As I but glance upon it all
Her path is lit by me
She walks where she chooses
She chooses me

You'll never have her now
I love her out of this world to the next and the next

Half a Star

For Laura G.

These hours only seem to pass
We must remember
We exist in this space between time
Our fingers entwined
Though miles of highway lay between us
I know strong Runes
To make the wheels roll
& pavement roll up at our feet
For without you
I am only half a star

Without you I am heartless
Walking over a bridge of human hearts
We tried, and we tried
We tried to make the serpents doves
Ruthless as gods we must be
Gods go!

Dwelt too long in the slums
Of the poor and sad
Chained to the gun in my hand
Imagined myself a Templar

My heart was pure
My Gospels corrupted
Betrayed by those I trusted
Who would bind me
And fill my mouth with sand

No slippery Jesus to save me
My heathen prayers drowned out
By angel's trumpets
I looked inward and found
My bindings like the breath of fish
I called to you, I have always called to you
You do not come - you GO to me
My red flame
Our union

Jim of the Roses

Jim had a garden
On top of the world
Roses, mums
Some other flowers?
You'd have to ask Jim

Jim had money from
Somewhere and he shared it
In this way
Up on that roof you owned
This town
Not the other way around

Jim got sick
Real sick but his family
Never came
A lifetime of collecting
Out on the streets
That's how I scored
All these books and a
Paisley shirt
I'll never wear

Jim of the roses

Is dead
And the mums and…
Asters?
The flowers are gone too
From the naked black tar
Rooftop
A skyline of daggers
Jab upwards
In anger

The Cyclist

The old man died
By the onion bins
Gripping my wrist
Open mouth
No air would come
Scream of silence

Heart attack
Head crack
What started as a claret halo
Pooled around us
On that monolithic floor
Glistening under humming lights
As if wrought of the frost
Of endless winter

Clacking carts of the
Marketing ladies
Pushed past
Not condescending to stop
They actually believed
They would escape with their
Pomegranates and pears

Bicycle clips
Narrowed dirty trouser legs
Now stilled
Grip released
I washed my hands
In the butcher's sink

Junkyard Song

Through the reeds
Past the warehouse
Lies the half eaten corpse
Of a deer
Fuel for feral dogs
Roaming irreclaimable parking lots

A mephitic stench rises
From unnatural channels
And their desultory deposits
Along these banks of the americas

Cratered blacktop holds pools
Of rainwater
Resplendent with motor oil
Rainbows
Strewn with ripped pages
Of pornographic magazines

On the hood of a dead automobile
I kiss you
The dress you bought on sale
Rips on metal
Obliquely jagged from some

Stranger's misfortune

Your highest heel kicks spasmodically
Against the radiator grill
Am I a man

A church bell sounds
In a far off town
Carried by tradewinds
To this valley of decay

Your head tips back
Your teeth clench
There is a tightness somewhere
A collapsing

Our love is pure
Uncut

Nothing on Earth

You're so defiant
On the surface
Your pride
Will be undone
Why stand defiant
On the surface?
It won't help you
Help me dig our tomb

The light you sought
Has found you
You have found
It is much too bright
You offer prayers
Then say it won't matter
The light dissolves you
Nothing on Earth remains

Desert sands crash down like rain
Why stand defiant
When nothing on Earth remains
Burning sands come down like rain
Won't be defiant
Nothing on Earth remains

Push back into the underground
Outside, it is much too bright
Impatient sands
Come to claim us
Dig down, dig deeper
Nothing unburied remains

So dark inside
Where I'm going
Miles, behind my eyes
Help me dig this tomb
Nothing unburied remains

So dark inside
Where I'm going
Miles, inside my mind
Help me dig this grave
Nothing on Earth remains

Go Street

This laundromat
Gets your grays grayer
Nights darker
This bodega
This brownstone
This purgatory

Unmarked cars float past
Doomed souls in knit caps
Cross 106th & Archeon
Unclean, unknowing
Corner of Amsterdam & Damnation

O what blow that phantom sold me
Cold ghost food
Empty rounds into empty guts
Empty head into sewer

Sonic horserace gentlemen
Who have lost everything
To the fury clouds

Every look, cough, twitch
Transaction

One cannot afford
Street life's semiotics
Codes of the broken
Vague vagaries
Memory and desire do not return only
Mockery and laughter
Summer's new shoes
Are too heavy to walk into heaven

Sounds never touch us

Shirtless men out windows
Twisting torsos on sooty sills
Whiskey men
Worm men
Infesting memorials to better days

Now comes some ghost
Throws skin coat over
Spectral shoulders
White van come
Door opens
Van go
Street
Gone

The Jackal and the Centipede

The jackal amuses herself
With a poisonous centipede
The fool
With a bottle of beer

Whose magnets pull down sympathies
Into her bell jar heart
Where lives no flame?

The boy, big and gangly
Shivers at the sound of mother's voice
Reading his medical history
Dream of life
Get bitten by a
Poisonous centipede

Breaking the wings of a cardinal
Clutching frequencies to her breast
Burning perspiration
Spitting death

Last this Century

Tonight we give you
The moon
A boxer's eye
Filling with blood

Imprint of our earth's shadow
Vision alive
With the hint of murder

Of the only real time
The anatomy of Christ
Spectacle too subtle
For neighbors asleep
In their aluminum huts
& minds

Dropping my spyglass
Returning to my dirty earth
& her surprises

Baby Grand

We're worried about
Baby's head

Its head is too large
It talks
It makes valid,
Insightful comments
It makes use of graphs and
Quantitative research

Its body so frail
Its head
So grotesque

So Below

Goodbye
Sick sky
I'm leaving you today
No longer will I keep you company

Nothing can grow
In the void of your shadow
Infinity revealed
A lonesome mirror

Cannot feel sad
At leaving
A sky should not feel small
& make me
Smaller

Bluebeard

I.

To look at me
Is to study darkness
Extinguish color
Rob from each hue
Coldness so cruel
All becomes blue

I only have served
As you asked me to do
I've carried your banner
Of bestial blue

Red-coated iron
Pressed to your palm
Is it a key
Or more of a pawn?
To open that chamber
Forbidden to you
Trespass against me
My room with no view

Too human the man

Whom lust corrupts
Fading mistress
Of the hollow king (I disown!)
Restored though he was
To blood-gemmed throne

All in the name
Of her invisible Lord
She held high his pennant
I sated my sword
Look upon me and see
My detestable face
A bloodline run dry
O! suicidal race

Does it pain you to know
There were others like you?
Where once beauty charmed
All becomes blue
You only shall see
What I want you to
Dead streams run together
And all becomes blue

II.

Was I strong too long
Was I ever strong
Too fast the fever
Got the cold feast

Were we strong too long
Were we ever strong
We became the night
Could not hold back
Coldness

& Cruelty

Sleep alone
Sleep cold
On waking
You will not recognize me

An empty hand
A closed heart
On returning
You will not welcome me

Was I strong too long

Did it ever help
Wake alone
Wake too late

An empty bed
A crossed heart
The promise of sleep
The solace of
Coldness

& Cruelty

Hellbender

Woefully drunk
Thrown from the tavern
Mutinous legs led me
To the mouth of a cavern
I followed a light
That soon disappeared
Hunger vexed
As evening shadows reared

Shambled for hours
Along a babbling river
Found a hellbender
For my dinner
Senses blurred
By these strange provisions
My mind bewildered
By terrible visions

A terrible beauty
Rode a terrible beast
Sang "All men come to me
From great to least"
She offered me her breast
I chose the one most near

From it flowed whiskey
The other, beer

"No longer shall you stand
With empty plate
If you but follow me
Through the gateless gate"

Upon her amber palm
I placed my fate
My lady, my beast
Of the gateless gate

Rags

Prone on the floor
This man
This dormant pile of oily rags
Will combust

It is hot
The man sweats
The walls sweat roaches
Outside, the street sweats bullets
Now and then one spirals
Into the condemned

Confined by fear
Defined by hate
This man
These burning rags

Plan "B"

Plan "B"
For revolution
Written in chalk
For the bored students
Who stare past it
To be erased in the morning
By the janitors

Damn the Dream

Joyless at the summer door
I smell grass
And nothing more
Children shoot rockets
Into the cool sky
The sky joyless as a whore

Damn the dream
Dream of stasis
Glued in place
A carnival ride
Going nowhere
I do not feel
Because I cannot feel
Joy
Damn the dream

Life Like

Johnny studied the scar
On his knee & swore it
Migrated an inch to
The left since last time
The white scar of more
Interest than the female form
On the bare concentration
Camp mattress

Rubbing his chin Johnny
Realized his cheap dinner
Masquerading as food
Was forcing its way
Through his pores & soon
His bowels
With cyanide speed

Johnny tired of self-examination
Initiated conversation
With the creature
Lying silent like
A battleship
Waiting

I Left

I left the window open
In flew an angel
Of death

He said
"Hello, I will come back
When you are done."

I said
"Can I have your number?"
It was on my head

I could read it in the mirror
The mirror turned black
 & cracked

Then the angel grabbed me
By my throat and said
"I will be back."

I closed the goddamn window

Sueños de Homicida

Trapped under white ceiling
Paint flaking sky
Choked with clouds
Demented frescoes
Scab poverty's cradle
Crude mottoes of shapeless children
Rotten mantras
Echo in streams of narial
Dream spray word violence

What listless seraph
Makes nests of shredded
Birth certificates
Clearing terrain in blasts
Of Santa Ana's cannons and
Gangster shotguns
Shoving souls into hot sky
Choked with loss

Two mongrels
One dead
Mouth dribble red yelping
Brute pain
His brother

Survivor
Guards his murdered heart
Crushed under the wheel

I imagine there is pity

World without Saints

Nothing bigger than us
In all creation?
Rejoice in the music
Of our sphere
Think we're rewarded
With temptation
There's nothing better
Than us here

A world without saints
Forgets how to pray
A life on the run
The kids have had their day
A world without saints
Forgets how to pray
Demand satisfaction
As we duel with The Way

Go to fists, go to guns
Defeat I AM
Pretend we rule
What we name
Stab the sky with steeples
Our church of man

But it's ourselves
We'll never tame

A world without saints
Forgets how to pray
Dance to the beat
Of the fallen angel band
A world without saints
Loses its way
And begs correction
From His whip hand

Disbelief won't keep us safe
Death comes leaping still
Bodies mortgaged
Souls on loan
Bridal veil, burial shroud
No triumph in our will
A world without saints
Forgets to atone

Hail the Coffin King!

I. The Carpenter

Sixty feet of pine
One quarter inch planed away
Onto packed dirt underfoot
Perfume of terpenes rising

Sweat darkens the elder's collarless work shirt
Staining it ivory
He adjusts his wire rims and saws into a board

"What ya makin' there old timer?"

My horror of trades masked
Poorly
Behind uneasy, feigned awe

The carpenter regards me
Without stopping his work
Calloused hands gesture
Towards an assembling mob

At their locus
A sinister youth

Twirling a wheelgun on
Slender forefinger

"Why, it's your coffin mister."

II. Ignoble

Dead meat in the belly
Dead meat in the womb
Weaned at a stinking shunt
Schooled in savagery
Your days a serial of
Weak moments

Blood rots in useless limbs
Now lie in drink
& wait for death
Drunk at her casket
Wishing you too
Were safe
In a box
Dead

III. Throttle Down

Choke Out
That last dying bloom
Choke out
With weed & thorn
Black out
That rose window
Black out!

Pull the lid
Shut on your coffin
And let no light in
Slam the door
On your mausoleum
And let no light in

Throttle Down!
& be unborn

Realize
Recognize you were never alive
Realize
Angels never sang your name
Resolve
To dissolve

Resolve
To let no other thought remain

Throttle Down!
That broken sun
That hazy light
Soulless heavens dim
Throttle Down!
The memory of pain
Of when you still felt pain
Of when you still
Felt

Your zodiac failure
Swastika sadness
Crucifix smile
Your tears and yearning
Of these
Nothing remains

& yet you ache?

IV. For the Bereaved

Lowered into the clay
Stuffed with sawdust and natron or
Exhausted cells dissipated
Above an industrial district
Bone gravel and cinders scraped up
Souvenirs

Should anyone love you then
Someone who loves you less might condole
"He's in a better place"
By which they will not mean
Disintegrating under a headstone or
Trapped like some slumbering djinn in brass
Eventually misplaced
On purpose under a cardboard box of
Christmas decorations in a dank nether

V. The Coffin King

For Drew K.

Who will help our brother?
Kyrie Eleison

It is a hard path
To the invisible horizon

What we see fail and fall
Serves only as his garment
What we feel
His undying firmament

His family, many brothers
Keep watch hour after hour
We are crew, we are true
Death has no power

Locked though we are
In this prison of fate
He gifts us his time
Though his hour is late

Help us remember
Your providence
In spite of mounting
Earthly evidence

And there it is!
His indomitable spirit
Though cancer wracked his body

He has valor to bear it

Into our hearts
He presses a key
To escape our fears:
Humility

Locked though he is
In his prison of fate
The strength of his spirit
Has broken the gate

Life is anything but fair
No one gets forever
A crown like Christ's waits
At the end of our tether

Thieves, you'll never take our friend
The Coffin King
We know death is not the end
For the Coffin King
We are raised from sleep's depths
With the Coffin King
We will survive this earthly death
Hail the Coffin King!

Spring Into Being

Heliotropic heads incline
Towards that majesty
Which sustains and gives
Their name
Whirling sphere feeds whirling disks
Flowers spiral within flowers
Beauteous symmetry, perfection
Angles irreducible illume
Magnificence of our Great
Arithmetician

If we seek
That living light
Will she bequeath
Such golden life?
Enthroned in her ratio
Our scepters root
In yielding loam

Night-capped heads awaken
Beatific faces warmed
By deathless rays
Tilt towards eternity
Returning the joy

In our spirits
Enkindled

As the vocalist for the legendary New York Hardcore Punk band Life's Blood, Jason O'Toole became known for his cutting, intelligent lyrics. O'Toole has relocated to the Boston, MA area after years of living in the American South where he worked as a police detective. A descendant of a "witch and paranormal" executed in New England, O'Toole has a calling to investigate the unknowable, recover lost traditions, and his poetry is informed by magick, folklore, and myth.